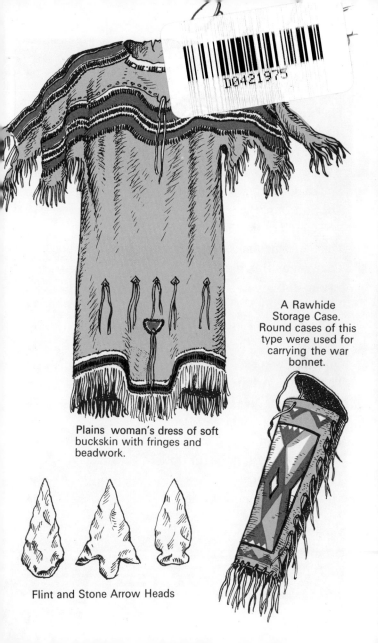

A Rawhide
Storage Case.
Round cases of this
type were used for
carrying the war
bonnet.

Plains woman's dress of soft
buckskin with fringes and
beadwork.

Flint and Stone Arrow Heads

INDEX

The story of the
INDIANS
of the Western Plains
written and illustrated
by FRANK HUMPHRIS

Ladybird Books Loughborough

The Plains Indians

Westward from the Mississippi River, the forests and hills of the eastern states of America gradually change to vast grass-covered prairies, rising to high, windswept plains. This great area, stretching hundreds of miles to the Rocky Mountains, was the home of the Plains Indians.

The most prominent of the many tribes were the Dakota (or Sioux — to give them the name by which they are usually known), the Cheyenne, Crow, Blackfoot, Arapahoe, Comanche and Kiowa. The Sioux were the largest and most powerful group. With their allies, the Cheyenne and the Arapahoe, they put up a tremendous struggle to keep their lands.

Although the language and customs of most of the tribes varied, the general way of life was very similar. There were some slight differences: for example, the Mandans and Pawnees, who lived in more or less permanent villages of large, dome-shaped, earth lodges, used the tepee only when on the move during the great seasonal hunts. The typical Plains Indians were nomads and hunters, living off the great buffalo herds and constantly on the move to new hunting grounds.

It was these bronzed warriors of the plains, notably the Sioux, hawk-nosed, tall and dignified in their feathered war bonnets and beaded costumes, who presented a picture of barbaric splendour which captured the imagination of the whole world.

Sioux Indians watch a wagon train
crossing their territory

The tepee

The typical dwelling, or lodge, of the Plains Indian was the conical skin tent known to us by the Sioux name, 'tepee'.

Tepees were made from buffalo hides, sewn together and supported on a framework of poles. For a nomadic people constantly on the move, tepees were both practical and comfortable. Sizes varied considerably. From ten to forty hides were required, depending on how large the lodge was to be. The average 'family' size was about 16 feet (4.87 m.) in diameter. The great 'council' or 'medicine'* lodges were much larger, one being recorded by a traveller in 1832 as measuring over 40 feet (12.19 m.) across.

The adjustable flaps at the top were a distinctive feature. These could be altered to control the ventilation and the upward current of air that carried the smoke through the opening. For added comfort an inner lining known as dew cloth, about four feet high, was tied to the poles inside. Its purpose was to keep out the draughts at ground level and, more important, to prevent rain water dripping from the poles in wet weather.

A small fire occupied the centre of the floor and around the walls were the robes used for bedding. Cooking utensils, rawhide containers, weapons and other implements completed the 'furnishing'. Tepee covers were often decorated with symbolic designs usually having some special meaning for the owner.

*the word 'medicine' referred to ceremonial ritual as well as a man's personal powers.

A village scene with tepees

The buffalo hunt

The life of the Plains Indian was almost entirely dependant on the existence of the buffalo. The great herds which roamed the plains provided the tribes with the main necessities of life — food, shelter and clothing.

Buffalo meat was rich and nourishing. From the hides came clothing, containers, tepee covers, cooking pots, rawhide for shields and ropes and — when tanned with the fur on — warm robes for bedding and winter wear. Horns, hoofs, bones and sinews were made into implements, tools, weapon points, glue and thread. Nothing was wasted.

The first big hunt of the year took place as the herds moved north, feeding on the fresh, spring grass. This was an important time, because tribes who had suffered a hard winter were often in need of food.

Because it was essential that the hunt be successful, a strict discipline was maintained in the camp. No-one was allowed to start prematurely and risk frightening a herd away. All had to act together.

The hunt itself was wild, exciting and dangerous. Mounted on their trained buffalo ponies, the men moved in for the kill, racing alongside the huge, shaggy beasts for a close-in lance thrust or arrow shot.

A skilful hunter could bring down several animals before the herd scattered too far. Then there was meat for all, for with many tribes it was a point of honour to share the food with the unsuccessful and old or needy.

A buffalo hunt was a great occasion
for a display of skill and courage

Buckskin and beadwork

The men were the hunters and the women had the task of curing and tanning the animal hides — and very hard work it was, too! Stretching, scraping, rubbing with mixtures of animal fat and brains, cleaning and softening, all took a great deal of time and labour. Deer, elk and antelope provided the finest buckskin for clothing, often so perfectly tanned that it was as soft as velvet. The heavier and coarser hides were used for other purposes.

Decoration was applied to almost everything. Formerly, this was achieved mainly by sewing dyed porcupine quills onto the buckskin with sinew thread. A high degree of artistic perfection was developed with the simple but effective designs.

Quillwork gradually declined as glass and china beads were introduced by Europeans during the 19th century. The bright, manufactured beads in many colours appealed to the Indians enormously and were a popular trading item. Highly elaborate embroidery became possible. Wide bands of beadwork embellished ceremonial war-shirts and leggings. Pipe bags, cradles, moccasins, robes, saddlebags, pouches and the head-bands on war bonnets were similarly decorated.

There were tribal differences both in the way the beads were sewn on and in the type of design. The Sioux, Cheyenne and Arapahoe patterns were typically geometric and these tribes used the 'lazy stitch' which gave a ridged appearance. The Crow and Blackfoot used the flat, 'overlaid' or 'spot stitch', which was more suitable to the floral shapes they incorporated in their designs.

An Indian woman preparing a hide for tanning. The skin is being 'fleshed' - that is, reduced to an even thickness by removing loose tissue with a scraper.

Plains Moccasins were made with soft uppers and rawhide soles.

Beaded Knife Sheath

Decorated Pipe Bag (Sioux)

Small pouches were worn on the belt and served as pockets.

The travois

When an Indian family travelled, their belongings were transported on a device known as a *travois*. This was a simple framework consisting of two, long tepee poles, the smaller ends of which were crossed over and fastened to the horse, leaving the butt ends dragging along behind.

Crossframes tied to the poles, and a network of rawhide strips, made a sort of platform on which were loaded heavy items such as the tepee covers, the robes used for bedding, and general camping gear.

Young children and the sick and aged could also be carried this way when necessary. Babies were usually on their mothers' backs, of course, safe in their cradle boards.

Personal articles, clothing and food were carried in *parfleches*, light, rawhide containers of various types. Some were packed on the travois, others were made in pairs to hang each side of the horse. A very common type was made from a sheet of rawhide folded rather like an envelope and fastened with thongs. Another type was cylindrical but this was used mainly for ritual objects. The smooth, rawhide surface of the parfleche was decorated with bold, geometric designs.

In the earlier days before the Indians obtained horses, dogs were used for transport. A small travois, but otherwise similar to that used with the horse, was harnessed to the dog's shoulders and on this a load of 60 lbs. (27 kgm.) or more, could be carried.

A tribe on the move, using the travois

Weapons of a warrior

From early childhood the young Indian boy was taught the skills and crafts he would need when he grew up and became a warrior. Probably almost the first 'toy' he played with was a miniature bow and arrow. As a man, the short, powerful bow became his main hunting weapon. It was usually about 3 ft. 6 ins. (106 cm.) in length for use on horseback and, on the better ones, thick animal sinew was glued to the back for added strength. Arrow points were made first of flint and stone, later of hoop iron when that became obtainable.

Next to the bow, the lance was the weapon most commonly used by the horsemen of the plains. Varying in length from eight to twelve feet, a lance was generally light, rather pliable, and often decorated with beaver and otter fur or with different kinds of feathers. Each would have a symbolic meaning for the owner.

The stone-headed club, made by shrinking rawhide round an oval stone and fastening it to a wooden handle, was popular with most Plains tribes. Various wooden clubs were also used. Of course, the iron axe-head of the tomahawk was obtained by trading.

To the warrior, the most important item in his equipment was his shield of thick, buffalo rawhide. Infinite care and patience, thought and prayer were bestowed upon it, for it was valued as much for the spiritual protection it gave its owner, as for its practical use as a means of defence. The designs and decorations were often revealed in visions and in these resided the medicine power of the shield.

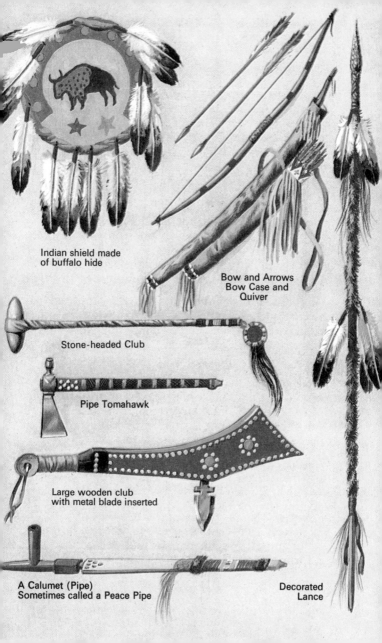

Indian shield made
of buffalo hide

Bow and Arrows
Bow Case and
Quiver

Stone-headed Club

Pipe Tomahawk

Large wooden club
with metal blade inserted

A Calumet (Pipe)
Sometimes called a Peace Pipe

Decorated
Lance

The eagle-feather war bonnet

Certain Plains tribes, the Sioux in particular, developed a form of 'feather heraldry' in which each feather denoted a brave deed. These 'coup' feathers, as they were called, may be compared to the campaign medals of the modern soldier, and the warrior's achievements could be recognised by the way the feathers were worn. From this developed the familiar war bonnet.

In the old days, tribal law allowed only the leading warriors with many war honours to wear war bonnets. Some of the more famous warriors won so many coup feathers in their lifetime, that a single or double tail of feathers was added and hung down the back. On page 21, Red Cloud is shown wearing a head-dress of this type.

Another form of bonnet consisted of a cap with a pair of horns attached, and a single, upright row of feathers running from the crown and forming a long tail. The cap was covered with ermine skins. At one time this style was seen as often as the other.

Eagle feathers were usually used by the Indians as representing the noblest and bravest bird. Neighbouring tribes of the Sioux wore similar head-dresses but did not always attach the same importance or meaning to the feathers.

The Blackfoot, for example, decorated their costumes with white weasel skins to indicate war honours. They favoured a bonnet with the feathers standing upright instead of sloping backwards in a wide flare (page 43).

Nowadays, most American Indians dress up in war bonnets on festive occasions, for this has been adopted as a form of national costume.

How eagles were trapped for their feathers

Eagles were sometimes caught by a pit trap baited with meat. As the eagle swooped it was grabbed by the legs and dragged into the hole.

The Sun Dance

One of the most important ceremonies common to almost all the Plains tribes was the Sun Dance. This was a great religious festival usually held in the spring, when the various nomadic bands of the tribe came together in one great gathering.

The ceremonies generally took place in a special enclosed area, around or facing a central pole. This pole, made from a tree trunk and decorated with symbolic objects, was chosen and erected with great solemnity. The dances were grave and extremely simple and often the performers went without food or drink for prolonged periods, hoping thereby to induce a trance-like state in which they might receive visions.

The ritual most associated with the Sun Dance was the spectacular self-torture practised by certain tribes, notably the Mandan, Sioux, Arapahoe and Cheyenne. The ordeal was undertaken for a variety of reasons. Young warriors, eager to prove their courage and manhood, submitted themselves to the test; with others it was a form of self-sacrifice to the spirits for favours either already received or hoped for in the future.

The participants had two parallel slits cut in the skin so that skewers could be inserted. Stout cords were attached at one end to the central pole and at the other to the skewers, and the dancers strained against the cords until they tore themselves loose.

Because of the torture aspect, the Government prohibited the Sun Dance about 1904 but removed the ban in 1935, having recognised the Indians' right to religious freedom. Since then, some tribes have revived the ceremony but in a very modified form.

The self-torture of the Sun Dance

Red Cloud of the Sioux

During the middle years of last century, Red Cloud rose to prominence as one of the great leaders of the Teton Sioux.

The Teton, or western division of the Sioux nation, consisted of five tribes, the Ogalallas, Unkpapas, Sans Arcs, Brulés and Minneconjous. Each tribe or clan was independant and had its own chief, who had gained his position by his own ability, for there were no hereditary titles among the Plains Indians.

Organisation was free and very democratic. A man who became a famous warrior, noted for his bravery, ability and character would attract a large number of followers and could in time become their chief. If he was a dominant personality with exceptional qualities, the other tribal groups would tend to follow his leadership in times of crisis. Such a man was Red Cloud, chief of the Ogalallas. For ten years he led the Sioux in a desperate struggle to keep their land from being overrun by the tide of western expansion.

In the illustration opposite Red Cloud is shown wearing the ceremonial war bonnet and costume, now preserved in the Buffalo Bill Museum at Cody, Wyoming. This shows the buckskin war-shirt, decorated with bands of beadwork over the shoulders and down the arms, with leggings, moccasins, and pipe bag similarly ornamented. The seams are trimmed with hair fringes. Shirts were not normally worn except on special occasions, the man's everyday dress being simply breech cloth and leggings. A robe or blanket covered the upper half of the body when necessary.

Chief Red Cloud in the ceremonial costume said to have been worn on a visit to the President of the United States

The Fetterman massacre

The land of the Teton Sioux had remained virtually undisturbed until the discovery of gold, in Montana territory, brought thousands of fortune seekers to the camps in the far west.

The Indians were alarmed and angered by the ever-increasing number of wagon trains crossing their hunting grounds, for the buffalo and deer were driven away from the neighbourhood of the trails. When the army began constructing a line of forts across the country, Red Cloud, then at the height of his power, led the tribes in an all out war against the intruders.

The main struggle was directed against Fort Phil Kearney. In the first five months, one hundred and fifty-four people were killed by the Sioux, twenty were wounded and nearly seven hundred head of livestock captured.

The wood-parties, cutting timber for building the fort were constantly attacked. One morning in December, 1866, violent signalling from a look-out announced that a wood train was again under attack.

The rescue party of seventy-nine soldiers and two scouts was put under the command of Captain Fetterman, a reckless officer with a contemptuous disregard for 'untrained savages'. His boast was that with eighty men he would ride through the whole Sioux nation. In spite of being warned by the fort commander not to pursue the Indians beyond Lodge Trail Ridge, Fetterman disobeyed orders and led his men directly into an ambush. Charging after a small group of picked warriors, the troops were surrounded by hundreds of Sioux and Cheyenne hidden in the trees and ravines.

Within a short time the whole command of eighty-one men were wiped out. Red Cloud's strategy was proving right!

Fetterman and his men being wiped out
by Red Cloud's warriors

The Wagon Box fight

Life at Fort Phil Kearney continued to be grim and dangerous. No-one was safe outside the stockade unless accompanied by a strong force of troopers, for Red Cloud kept a determined grip on the fort.

His next major assault was directed against a company of woodcutters and hauliers working about five miles from the post.

Captain Powell, in charge of the escort, ordered the hauliers' heavy wagon boxes to be removed from the wheel bases and placed in a rectangular formation for defence. As hundreds of Indians massed on the surrounding heights, the little group of thirty-two white men prepared to make every shot a deadly one.

The first burst of fire from the corral brought many of the charging warriors crashing to the ground, but the rest kept on, confident that they would over-run the corral while the defenders paused to reload. To their consternation there was no pause in the firing. A constant stream of flame and lead came from the wagon boxes, breaking the charge and forcing the Indians to retire.

Unknown to the Sioux, new breech-loading rifles capable of sustained rapid fire had been issued to the troops in place of the old, slow muzzle-loaders.

To the Indians the constant firing was simply unbelievable. Again and again that day and with the utmost bravery they attempted to reach the corral, only to be driven back with heavy losses until, shocked and disheartened, they withdrew.

To lose so many of his finest warriors was a heavy blow to Red Cloud's prestige. However, he grimly held to his purpose until finally a new treaty was drawn up in which the Government agreed to recall the troops and abandon the forts that had been the cause of so much bloodshed.

The new breech-loading rifles bring Red Cloud's warriors to a halt

Sitting Bull

The battle of the Little Big Horn, a disaster for the American military, was fought on June 25th, 1876, and from that day the name of Sitting Bull, the Sioux chief, became a part of western history.

There are differing versions of the precise role played by Sitting Bull at the battle. Some say he was away making 'medicine' — others that he was there and fought with the rest. Whichever is correct, there is no doubt it was his organising ability that gathered the tribes together in readiness for the struggle he knew would come. It was he who had a vision that correctly foretold the result of the battle. For by this time he was more of a 'medicine man', an astute political leader, than a fighting chief.

To the shocked American public, however, the only explanation seemed to be that General Custer had ridden into a clever trap prepared by a cunning Indian named Sitting Bull.

There had been no trap and the huge Indian encampment was not hidden. It spread over a valley between hills, and Custer attacked it and lost the battle through over-confidence and the wrong tactics.

After the battle, Sitting Bull escaped into Canada with his followers but returned to the States in 1881 and surrendered. He spent about two years as a prisoner, then about 1885 he toured with Buffalo Bill's Wild West Circus where he was the main attraction.

For the rest of the time he lived on the Standing Rock Reservation. From his cabin he could look out at the great land around him and remember the days when it all belonged to his people.

The Cheyenne

Throughout the years of warfare in the West, hardly a battle took place that did not include at least some of the 'fighting Cheyenne'. They were with Red Cloud at the Fetterman and Wagon Box fights, and a large number took part in the battle of the Little Big Horn.

However, the defeat of Custer's Seventh Cavalry was the last great victory for the Indians on the northern plains. Following the battle, strong forces of U.S. troops took the field, pursuing and inflicting crushing defeats, one after another, on the various Indian villages.

The northern Cheyenne suffered heavily and were forced to surrender after their winter camp was attacked and all the lodges, food and clothing destroyed. They were promised a reservation in the north. Instead they were sent nearly a thousand miles south, to an area so unhealthy that within a year many were dead from fever and starvation. The rest, sick, hungry and in rags, realised that before long they would all be dead, and repeatedly asked the authorities to be allowed to return to their own land.

At last their patience gave out. In July, 1878, Little Wolf, the fighting chief, expressed the feelings of his people when he told the agent, "I am going to leave here. I am going north to my own country. I do not want to see blood spilt about this agency. If you are going to send soldiers after me, let me get a little distance from the agency. Then if you want to fight I will fight you and we can make the ground bloody at that place."

Little Wolf tells of the feelings of his people and his wish to avoid bloodshed

Dull Knife and Little Wolf march home

Of the three hundred or so Cheyenne who started their epic journey to the north, only about eighty were fighting men. The rest were old men, women and children. Ahead of them were hundreds of miles of open country with military forces, forts and artillery, ranchers, cowboys, miners and frontier communities, all ranged against one small group of Indians!

Little Wolf's first need was for horses and arms. Scattered raids on farms and ranches brought in a sufficient number of horses, and here and there the warriors managed to pick up rifles and ammunition. Several times during that extraordinary march they were attacked by pursuing soldiers, but always they fought them off and hurried onwards. A large force of soldiers from Fort Dodge was forced to withdraw with their Colonel dead. In some incredible way the Indians kept on, avoiding conflict where possible but fighting with desperate courage each time they were attacked.

Once beyond the North Platte River, the old chief, Dull Knife, felt he was home and would go no further. Many others, exhausted by the long journey, agreed with him. Little Wolf and his followers were determined to continue and so, sadly, the two groups parted.

In late October, Dull Knife and his people were found by the cavalry in the sand hills of Nebraska. They were a pitiful spectacle. Ragged, thin and suffering from the cold they surrendered and were taken to Fort Robinson to await the Government's decision.

Like ghosts the Cheyenne drift past an army outpost,
avoiding conflict

The last of the Cheyenne

The tragic events at Fort Robinson were a horrifying example of what can happen through mistaken policies and misunderstanding.

At first the Indians were treated kindly and had a fair degree of freedom, while the telegraph was busy with messages and instructions to and from Washington as to their final destination.

Some weeks later the decision was made. The Indians must return to the south. Dull Knife replied, "You may kill us here but we will never go back." Argument and persuasion had no effect. An exasperated Captain Wessells now kept the prisoners locked in the barracks and cut off their food and water hoping this would make them agree to move. The answer was the same — they would rather die than go back.

On a bitterly cold night in January the Cheyenne overpowered the guards, took their rifles and ammunition, broke out of the barracks and fled across the deep snow towards the bluffs. The soldiers were soon after them. By morning, many Indians too weak to run far, had been recaptured or killed — fifty were found frozen to death in the snow. It was several days before all were accounted for. Sixty-four Cheyenne had been killed and seventy-eight recaptured for the loss of eleven soldiers killed and ten wounded.

The warriors with Little Wolf were more fortunate. The following year they were discovered by the army, but policies had changed and eventually they were given a reservation in Montana. They had come home.

*The unhappy and homesick Cheyenne
break out of captivity in Fort Robinson*

Quanah Parker

No-one in the Texas settlement of Parker's Fort dreamed of trouble on a May morning in 1836. The settlement was strongly built, and there had been no Indian raids in that area for so long that people became careless. Many slept in the cabins on their outlying farms rather than in the fort. The sudden fury of the Comanche attack caught them all unprepared and most of the inhabitants were killed.

Mrs. Kellog, Mrs. Plummer with her baby son, and two children — nine-years-old Cynthia Ann Parker and her brother John — were taken prisoner and carried off by the Comanches. The two women were eventually ransomed and returned to civilization. But Cynthia Ann did not escape. Twenty years after the massacre at Parker's Fort, a force of U.S. dragoons captured a Comanche village and found there a blue-eyed woman with fair hair. It was Cynthia Ann Parker, then the wife of chief Peta Noconi and mother of his children.

Her eldest son, Quanah, grew to be chief of the Comanches and one of the leading dare-devils whose war-parties kept the frontier in turmoil.

Cynthia Ann was taken back to her relatives but had become so Indian that she could not reconcile herself to the white man's ways and died within a few years.

The fight at Adobe Walls

By 1874 many of the great herds of buffalo that once roamed the plains in their millions had been wiped out by the white man. It was the most appalling slaughter of animals the world has ever seen — and the most wasteful, for only the hides were taken — the carcases were left to rot on the plains.

This wanton killing brought despair to the Indians. To them it meant starvation. Day after day, as their scouts went out in search of the herds that were no longer there, their hatred of the white man increased. The hide hunters were attacked whenever they were found.

One such attack took place at Adobe Walls, in the Texas Panhandle. Under cover of night a large force of Comanches, led by Quanah Parker, came up to the buildings where a number of white men were sleeping. Only a fortunate accident awakened them in time.

It was an awe inspiring and fearsome sight that met their eyes as the feathered, war-painted warriors swept down in the cold light of dawn. The Indians rode right to the very doors, but the men in the huts were no settlers or farmers—they were experienced frontiersmen, every man a crack shot with the big bore Sharps' rifle which brought the Indians down as efficiently as it had the buffalo.

The Indian losses were heavy. Bravery was not enough — they had no answer to such a powerful long range weapon in the hands of determined men.

With this defeat Quanah realised the old way of life was ending for ever. He sought out his mother's people and with their help came to terms with the changing frontier. "If she could learn the ways of the Indian," he said, "I can learn the ways of the white man."

36   *Quanah leads the despairing tribes against the buffalo hunters who were bringing them near to starvation*

Joseph of the Nez Percé

One of the most remarkable Indians in the history of the West was Joseph, chief of the Nez Percé tribe, an intelligent and advanced people whose homeland lay far to the northwest of the Sioux. For half a century they had been at peace with the white people until the Government decided to open their beautiful valley to white settlers and place the Nez Percé on a reservation.

Under the pressure of being forced from their homes, the anger of this peaceful tribe reached breaking point. Trouble erupted and a number of settlers were killed. Troops were ordered out to punish the Indians and bring them in to a reservation.

Joseph moved his village to White Bird Canyon and, by clever defensive tactics, almost annihilated the attacking soldiers. War was now inevitable.

Stronger forces under General Howard moved against Joseph, who realised that the only way he could save his people was to keep ahead of the troops and eventually try to reach Canada.

This amazing retreat in which men, women and children, and even the elderly, took part, covered approximately one thousand eight hundred miles and can only be regarded as an extraordinary military achievement.

Joseph, who had never fought a battle in his life, proved to be a tactical genius, capable of handling his small fighting force with such great skill that the veteran army commanders opposing him were outfought and out-manoeuvred time and again.

From all directions the troops came, some five thousand in all. Two thousand of these were actually met in battle by Joseph's three hundred warriors.

Heavily outnumbered, the Indian braves protect the women, children and elderly trying to reach the Canadian Frontier

The surrender of the Nez Percé

It was exhaustion and hunger that forced Joseph to halt when only thirty miles from the Canadian border and safety. Horses and humans could go no further without rest. Far behind were the forces of General Howard. General Gibbon's troops had been fought to a standstill though at the cost of eighty-nine Indian lives, fifty of whom were women and children. The 7th Cavalry were also out of the fight with numerous casualties.

It was now October and bitterly cold. The Nez Percé had fought and retreated for four incredible months. Only seventy fighting men remained alive, half of them wounded. It seemed to Joseph that it would be safe to relax, but the delay proved fatal.

Unknown to the chief, fresh troops under General Miles had found their trail, and once again the weary Nez Percé found themselves under attack. After a two-day battle in which artillery was used against the Indians, Joseph finally surrendered to save further bloodshed.

His speech was moving and infinitely pathetic. "I am tired of fighting," he said. "Our chiefs are killed. The old men are all dead. It is cold and we have no blankets. The little children are freezing to death. I want to have time to look for my children and see how many I can find; maybe I shall find them among the dead. Hear me my chiefs, my heart is sick and sad. From where the sun now stands I will fight no more, forever!"

Joseph never saw his beloved homeland again. He died suddenly in 1904—probably from a thrombosis. At the time his friends used a less clinical but more understanding phrase. They said he died from a broken heart.

Joseph makes his moving speech of surrender

The Blackfoot

The Blackfoot were a powerful group of three warrior tribes inhabiting the plains of southern Alberta in Canada, and northern Montana in the United States. The group comprised the Pikuni, or Piegan (pronounced 'Pay-gan'), the Kainah, or Blood, and the Siksika or Blackfoot proper, sometimes referred to as the northern Blackfoot. All three tribes spoke the same language, observed similar customs and were typical of the nomadic, buffalo hunting Plains Indians. They were constantly at war with their neighbours.

To the west their country was safeguarded by the Rocky Mountains but to the east were the hostile Cree and Assiniboin, while on their southern front were their traditional enemies, the Crow and Shoshone.

The Blackfoot were at the height of their power about 1830 when an outbreak of the dreaded small-pox killed nearly half their number. Further outbreaks, followed by near starvation when the buffalo were gone, broke their power completely and they came under government control. Today the Blackfoot live on reservations situated in areas of their old hunting grounds in Alberta and Montana.

In the illustration an old chief is shown wearing the traditional bonnet of the Blackfoot. This had a crown of vertical feathers, the cap being decorated with brass studs and white weasel skins.

Blackfoot beadwork is distinguished by geometric designs incorporating a number of small squares arranged in rectangles and triangles. Later, simple flower and leaf patterns were introduced as shown on the old chief's gauntlets.

A Blackfoot chief in full costume

The Blackfoot and the fur trade

The first white people with whom the Blackfoot came in contact, after the early explorers, were the trappers and fur traders. Even among these tough and hardy adventurers the Blackfoot had a reputation for savage and relentless warfare.

Many other Indian tribes had proved friendly—at least at first—to the trappers, being eager to obtain the white man's trade goods. But not so the Blackfoot. They were liable to attack anyone who entered their lands.

However, even the Blackfoot found that trade was sometimes necessary, particularly when hostile Cree and Assiniboin Indians, armed with guns, began to raid their territory.

The guns had been obtained from traders further east around the Hudson Bay and Great Lakes area. Two English trading companies were therefore allowed to build posts on the Saskatchewan River in Blackfoot country, and in general the Indians got on fairly well with the English and Canadian traders, but not with the Americans! This was partly due to the fact that American trappers came from the south-east, the same direction as the bitter enemies of the Blackfoot, the Crows and Shoshone.

Moreover, the Americans were known to be on very friendly terms with the latter tribes. Whenever possible they were attacked and their furs stolen and taken back into Canada for barter at the trading posts.

Unlike other Indian tribes the Blackfoot never engaged in a formal war with the white man. The advancing white frontier largely by-passed them to the south, while in Canada the progress of assimilation was gradual and comparatively peaceful.

A trading post

The Ghost Dance

By the late 1880s the Indians were herded into reservations and living on food and clothing doled out by the agencies. Both were inadequate.

In this time of bitterness and despair, rumours began to circulate of a new religion. Far away in Nevada a young Painte named Wovoka claimed to have had a revelation that all the dead Indians were about to return to the earth, that the Plains would be black with buffalo again, and that the old days of glory would return. He combined this doctrine with a pacifist policy prohibiting warfare and urging all to love one another. It was a strange mixture of Christian and pagan beliefs.

Wovoka also taught his people a dance which was to bring about these wonders. From one tribe to another the idea spread. Everywhere the Indians were dancing, many until they fell into a trance and believed they talked with the spirits. For this reason the dance became known as the Ghost Dance.

The Sioux embraced this new religion with particular fervour. To them it seemed to mean that the white man would be exterminated with the help of the spirit warriors. An Indian Messiah was coming!

Considerable alarm was now felt among the towns and cities of the plains. An Indian outbreak seemed imminent, and troops were hastily mobilised. At this moment of high tension, Sitting Bull began to show an interest in the movement. Fearful of the result if the famous chief took an active part, the authorities ordered his arrest, but a fight developed and Sitting Bull was shot—ironically by an Indian policeman, one of his own tribe. So died a great Sioux leader!

Massacre at Wounded Knee

Sitting Bull was killed on December 15th, 1890. With his death many of his followers left the reservation and fled south to join Big Foot's band of 'wild' Indians. While some still believed in the Messiah and continued the Ghost Dance, other groups, growing apprehensive of the troops now closing in from all directions, submitted quietly and returned to the agencies. But a large number, possibly two or three thousand, inflamed by the continuous dancing, were concentrating in the Dakota Bad Lands.

The military were ordered to round up all Indians outside the reservations and disarm them, and this was the situation when Big Foot's band was intercepted near Wounded Knee Creek by units of the 7th Cavalry. The following morning, December 29th, the search for arms began. Everyone could feel the tension.

Whether an Indian or a white man fired first no-one knows, but at the sound of a shot the soldiers fired point blank into the groups of Indians, who fought desperately. From the surrounding heights four Hotchkiss cannon opened up with 2 lb. explosive shells. Within minutes over two hundred Sioux, men, women and children and sixty soldiers were killed and wounded. A fierce blizzard ended the fight. When the troops returned to the scene many of the dead were found grotesquely frozen where they had fallen. The Ghost Dance scare was over—it was the last bitter spark of resistance on the Plains.

Despairing and sick at heart the remaining Sioux were slowly pushed back to the reservations. For the Indian it was the final, tragic end of the old way of life.

After the battle Chief Big Foot is found frozen in the snow

The Indian today

The majority of the Plains Indians now live on reservations situated on the old tribal lands. These vary considerably in size, some being quite small while ten, at least, have over a million acres each.

Although poverty is still a major problem among many groups, an increasing number of Indians are now engaged in stock-raising, farming and the timber industry. Others find seasonal employment on ranches and in local industrial projects. But the Indian has been, and still is, slow in adjusting to the white man's ways. Many have no desire to do so—why should they? They regard as unnecessary so many of the things the white man thinks are essential for happiness.

Since the early days many changes have been made by the administration in the handling of Indian affairs. Thanks mainly to the efforts of men and women devoted to Indian welfare, new laws have replaced old ones found to be unsatisfactory, and today the Indian can look forward to a greater understanding between the two races.

American citizenship was extended to all Indians in 1924; they also have the same right to vote as other U.S. citizens and pay the same taxes, except on lands held in trust by the Government. Many fought with distinction in both world wars.

Indian men and women hold responsible posts at various levels of state and federal government—but these are the minority. On the great reservations large numbers still live more or less traditionally, maintaining the customs and taboos of their ancestors as far as they can; proud of the fact that they are Indians.

INDIAN TRIBES of the PLAINS AND SURROUNDING AREAS

SHOWING THE LOCATION OF THE MAIN INDIAN RESERVATIONS AT THE PRESENT TIME

INDIAN RESERVATIONS

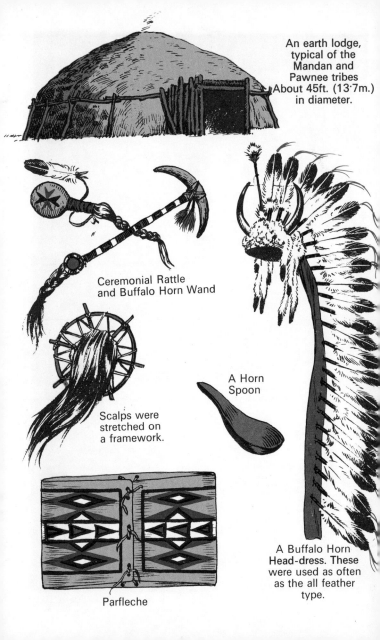

An earth lodge, typical of the Mandan and Pawnee tribes About 45ft. (13·7m.) in diameter.

Ceremonial Rattle and Buffalo Horn Wand

Scalps were stretched on a framework.

A Horn Spoon

Parfleche

A Buffalo Horn Head-dress. These were used as often as the all feather type.